THE PENTECOSTAL SHAMAN

A Journey of Healing, Spiritual Awakening, and Divine Power

Jeffrey Craig McClure

Copyright © 2024

All rights reserved

No part of this book may be reproduced, stored in a retrieval system, or transmitted in any form or by any means, electronic, mechanical, photocopying, recording, or otherwise, without the prior written permission of the publisher, except for brief quotations embodied in critical articles and reviews.

Contents

Introduction: Awakening the Light Within 1

Chapter 1: A Soul With No Identity 3
    Childhood curiosity and feeling out of place
    Early encounters with faith and unanswered prayers
    Realizing questions are a compass for deeper purpose

Chapter 2: A Legacy of Faith and Music 6
    Growing up in a family of ministers and musicians
    The church as both sanctuary and stage
    Music as a connection to divine presence

Chapter 3: Religious Trauma aka Church Hurt 8
    Betrayal and disillusionment in the church
    Speaking out against spiritual abuse
    Beginning the journey of questioning faith

Chapter 4: My Journey into the Spiritual Planes 12
    Vivid dreams and supernatural encounters
    Discovering spiritual authority through fear
    Lessons from the unseen realms

Chapter 5: The Astral Plane and Lessons of Fear 21
    Experiencing the astral plane and its challenges
    Confronting dark entities with divine power
    Transforming fear into spiritual growth

Chapter 6: The Pentecostal Shaman 25
    Embracing a dual identity as a Pentecostal and a shaman

Bridging traditional faith with mystical practices

Walking in divine love and spiritual authority

Chapter 7: Miracles Across Planes 29

Understanding miracles as a natural expression of divine love

Testimonies of healing and transformation

Aligning with faith, love, and intention

Chapter 8: Seraphim's Flame 33

Encounter with a seraphim and receiving the Divine Fire

Learning to wield the flame for healing and protection

Using the fire to guide others toward liberation

Chapter 9: The Power of Questioning God 37

Embracing doubts as a path to deeper faith

Breaking free from the limitations of rigid doctrine

Discovering the divine through personal exploration

Chapter 10: Healing Trauma 41

The impact of trauma on the soul and spirit

Confronting wounds and reclaiming lost soul fragments

Forgiveness as a tool for liberation and healing

Chapter 11: Full Circle – Returning to Love and Service .. 46

Re-entering the church with a new perspective

Serving others through love and spiritual gifts

Finding forgiveness and purpose in past wounds

Chapter 12: Awakening to Your Divine Potential 50

Recognizing the divine light within yourself

Overcoming fear and stepping into spiritual authority

   Living in alignment with your infinite potential

Conclusion:

   Embracing the sacred journey of awakening

   Walking in love, light, and divine power

   Continuing the path of discovery and transformation

Introduction
Awakening the Light Within

From the moment I could form thoughts, I knew there was more to life than what I could see with my physical eyes. My questions began early, small but profound: *Why am I here? What is my purpose?* Over time, they grew louder, unrelenting, driving me to search for answers in places both familiar and strange.

I was born into a lineage of preachers and musicians, steeped in the rhythm of church life and the comforting cadence of scripture. For generations, my family carried the torch of faith, and it burned brightly within me—until the very institution I trusted as my foundation revealed its flaws. The church, which had been my sanctuary, became the source of some of my deepest wounds. Betrayal, disillusionment, and the weight of unanswered prayers nearly shattered me.

Yet, it was in this breaking that I found something extraordinary.

Through heartache, spiritual battles, and moments of transcendent revelation, I began to see the divine in a way I had never been taught. My journey led me beyond the boundaries of traditional faith, into realms where angels and demons dwell, where healing and miracles are not just stories but lived experiences. It was in these moments, in the places where faith met the mystical, that I began to reclaim the truth of who I was: a healer, a seeker, a warrior of light.

This book is my story—a testimony of transformation and a guide for those who feel trapped in the shadows of doubt, fear, or religious dogma. It's for the ones who ask questions that others are afraid to voice, for those who feel they don't belong, and for those who hunger for a connection with the divine that transcends tradition.

I share my experiences not as an authority or a perfect soul, but as a fellow traveler on the path. Together, we will walk through my battles with the unseen, my encounters with angels and darkness, and the profound lessons I learned along the way. This is a story of liberation, healing, and awakening to the infinite power within.

As you read, I invite you to step into your own truth. This is not just my journey—it is an invitation to begin yours. To question. To heal. To awaken. The divine light you seek is already within you. My prayer is that, through these pages, you will find the courage to discover it for yourself.

Chapter 1
A Soul With No Identity

From as early as I can remember, I felt like a stranger even to my own family. It wasn't a dramatic feeling, but a quiet, persistent sense that I was out of synch with the world around me. While other children laughed, played, and seemed content to live in the moment, I was consumed by a relentless curiosity about life's deeper questions.

Who was I? What was my purpose? Why did the world feel so disconnected from the truth I sensed somewhere just beyond my reach?

At the time, I couldn't articulate these thoughts. I only knew that I saw the world differently. Adults often called me an "old soul," but their words didn't give me a sense of direction—they only deepened my feelings of isolation.

My family's faith was a central part of my upbringing. My father, a pastor and musician, was the heart of our household, and his devotion to the church shaped everything we did. Sundays were spent in the pews, evenings were filled with scripture and song, and our lives revolved around the rhythms of worship. Our family carried a legacy of ministry, with preachers and musicians spanning generations. To my father, our calling was sacred—an inheritance from God that had been passed down like a divine torch.

The church was my first world, and it was a world filled with awe and wonder. I remember sitting in the pews as a child, watching the congregation lift their hands in praise, their faces aglow with joy and surrender. I marveled at the moments when the Holy Spirit would sweep through the room, leaving people trembling, weeping, or speaking in tongues. To a child's eyes, it was magic—a glimpse of something holy and untouchable.

But for all the wonder around me, I struggled to feel it for myself. I longed to experience the presence of God in the way others did, to feel the warmth of divine love wash over me. I prayed earnestly, desperately: *God, I want to feel You. I want to know You.*

Yet, no matter how fervently I prayed, God always felt just out of reach.

By the time I was seven, this yearning had turned into a constant companion. I remember kneeling by my bed one night, tears streaming down my face, as I asked God why I couldn't feel Him the way others seemed to. I wanted to understand why I felt so different, why the world around me felt like a mask hiding something greater, something unseen.

As I grew older, my hunger for answers only intensified. I pored over the Bible, searching for the mysteries of life within its pages. I read stories of healing, miracles, and resurrection, and I wanted desperately to believe that such things were still possible. I believed that casting out demons, raising the dead, and bringing wholeness to the broken was still possible, even though I had not witnessed that with my own eyes. But as the years passed, my prayers for purpose seemed to go unanswered. The God I sought remained elusive, a distant figure whose love I couldn't quite grasp.

What I didn't realize then was that my longing for connection was not a flaw—it was my compass. The questions that kept me awake at night, the sense of not belonging, the insatiable hunger for truth—these were not signs of weakness. They were the seeds of something greater, the beginning of a journey that would take me far beyond the walls of the church.

Looking back, I understand that the answers I sought were never meant to come easily. They were buried in the soil of struggle, waiting to be unearthed through the trials that would test and refine me. The questions that haunted me as a child were the same questions that would one day lead me to discover my purpose.

But before I could find my answers, I would have to tread through the fire.

Chapter 2
A Legacy of Faith and Music

Faith wasn't just something we practiced in my family—it was who we were. For generations, the rhythms of gospel music and the echo of sermons had coursed through my family's veins, weaving a legacy as undeniable as the color of our skin. To us, ministry wasn't just a calling; it was a birthright, passed down from my great-grandfather, who first stood at the pulpit with trembling hands and a heart ablaze with conviction.

My father embodied this legacy. A pastor and a gifted musician, he carried the weight of our family's spiritual inheritance with unwavering devotion. I often watched him at the organ, his fingers dancing over the keys, coaxing melodies that seemed to pull heaven closer. His sermons, delivered with a mix of authority and grace, filled the sanctuary with a palpable sense of hope. He was a man of faith, and his belief in God's power was evident.

The church was both a sanctuary and a stage, a place where my family's gifts shone brightest. Music was central to our worship, and it was through music that I first began to understand the power of connection. I remember sitting at the organ for the first time, my feet barely reaching the bass pedals, as my father guided my hands across the keys. The sound that emerged wasn't perfect, but it was powerful—an offering, raw and unrefined, that stirred something deep within me.

In my teens, I began to take on more responsibilities in the church. I became the church organist, a role that filled me with both pride and purpose. Sitting at the organ, I felt a connection to something larger than myself, a sense of belonging that eluded me in other areas of my life. I played not just to fill the space with sound but to invite the Holy Spirit into the room, to create an atmosphere where miracles felt possible.

Yet, even in those sacred moments, a part of me remained restless. I loved the church, but I couldn't ignore the undercurrent of questions that ran through my mind. Why did God seem so close to others but so distant to me? Why did the rituals of faith sometimes feel more like performance than connection? And why, despite my best efforts, did I still feel like an outsider in the one place I was supposed to belong?

The church was my home, but it was also a place of contradictions. It was where I first felt the presence of God, but it was also where I began to sense the cracks in the foundation of my faith. It was where I learned to love, but also where I would come to know betrayal. It was a place of healing and a place of hurt, a paradox that would shape the rest of my journey.

Through it all, the music remained. It was my anchor, my refuge, my way of reaching for the divine even when words failed me. And as I played, I began to understand that the legacy of faith and music I had inherited was not just a gift—it was a calling. But what that calling would ultimately demand of me, I could never have imagined.

Chapter 3
Religious Trauma aka Church Hurt

For all its beauty and power, the church was not immune to imperfection. As I grew older, the church became a place of contradictions. It was where I learned to sing hymns of hope and forgiveness, yet it was also where I first encountered betrayal and judgment. The place that had nurtured my soul became a battleground for my faith.

It started subtly, with whispers and sideways glances. I noticed the cracks in the walls of the institution long before I fully understood what they meant. The sermons that once inspired me began to feel rehearsed, hollow, as if the passion behind them had faded into routine. The people I looked up to, the leaders of faith who had once seemed larger than life, began to show their humanity in ways that were hard to ignore.

Then came the betrayal that shattered the illusion completely. When I reached the age of 18, I accepted my calling as the minister of music at a neighboring church. While there, I looked to that church's ministers for guidance and wisdom, trusting them to help me navigate the complexities of life and faith. But that trust was broken when I became the target of inappropriate sexual advances from several of the male ministers—men who had taken vows to serve God and the community with integrity.

At first, I couldn't believe what was happening. I was naive, unable to comprehend that those in positions of spiritual authority could exploit their power. The weight of their actions left me feeling confused, ashamed, and deeply betrayed. When I finally found the courage to speak up, I expected support, understanding, and justice. Instead, I was met with rumors and blame.

The same community that had preached love and acceptance turned on me. They whispered that I was at fault, that I had somehow invited the advances. Some even accused me of manipulating the situation for attention. The hurt was unbearable. The church, which had been my haven, now felt like a prison. The people I had trusted with my soul seemed more concerned with preserving their reputations than seeking the truth.

A seed of anger was planted in my heart that day, and with it, a deep skepticism toward the institution that had once been my sanctuary. I began to question everything I had been taught: Was this what faith truly looked like? Was God present in a place where injustice and hypocrisy thrived? And if the church wasn't what I thought it was, then where did that leave me?

Around this time, my spiritual gifts began to awaken in ways I couldn't ignore. I started having more vivid dreams and visions, experiencing encounters with angels and battling demons in the unseen realms. These experiences were both awe-inspiring and terrifying, and they left me grappling with questions I couldn't ask anyone in the church. How could I reconcile these supernatural encounters with the brokenness I saw in the institution that claimed to represent God?

The Bible spoke of "rightly dividing the word of truth" (2 Timothy 2:15), and I realized that this was what I had to do—not just with scripture, but with my entire understanding of faith. I had to sift through the teachings I had been given, separating the divine essence from the human flaws that had tainted it. It was a painful process, one that required me to let go of the church as I had known it and begin a new chapter of my journey.

For a time, I turned away from the church entirely. I rejected everything I had been taught, everything I thought I knew about God and faith. I needed to start from scratch, to strip away the layers of doctrine and tradition that no longer served me. In this season of searching, I prayed a prayer that would change the course of my life forever:

"I am lost, and I don't know which way to go. God, Jesus, Great Spirit, Creator—whatever You are, whoever You are—please reveal to me the truth. Strip away everything from me that is a lie, and fill me only with truth."

This prayer marked the beginning of a profound transformation. It was an invitation for true love to lead me—not through the voices of preachers or the pages of doctrine, but through personal revelation and experience. What I didn't realize was that this journey would take me beyond the boundaries of traditional faith, into realms I had never imagined.

In the years that followed, I began to see the divine in a new way. I encountered the Holy Spirit not as a distant force but as a living, breathing presence that moved within and around me. I discovered truths that transcended the limitations of religion, truths that spoke to the essence of who I was and what I was meant to do.

The trials I faced in the church were not the end of my story—they were the catalysts for a deeper, more expansive understanding of faith. They forced me to confront the shadows within myself and within the institution, to seek the light that had always been there, hidden beneath the surface.

Looking back, I can see that these trials were not meant to destroy me but to refine me. They stripped away the illusions I had clung to, forcing me to build my faith on a foundation of truth rather than tradition. And in that process, I found something far greater than I ever could have imagined.

Chapter 4
My Journey into the Spiritual Planes

The first time I experienced the spiritual planes, I didn't know what to make of it. It wasn't a gentle introduction or a fleeting glimpse; it was a full immersion into a world that felt more vivid and alive than anything I'd known in waking life. At first, I thought it was my imagination playing tricks on me, but the experiences were too real, too profound to dismiss. They left me in awe—and in turmoil.

It began with dreams that felt more like memories. I would wake up drenched in sweat, the echoes of battles with unseen forces still ringing in my ears. At night, I found myself standing in places that seemed both familiar and otherworldly, places where angels and demons waged wars that I could not fully understand. These weren't just dreams; they were lessons, though I didn't realize it at the time.

One night, I dreamed of standing in an open field bathed in purple and silver light. The air was thick with love, and I could feel the presence of something vast and powerful just beyond my sight. Suddenly, a figure emerged—a being of light, its form radiant and barely contained within its shape. It looked at me, and though it didn't speak, I understood its message: *Many are called, but you are Chosen.*

At the time, I didn't know what that meant. Called to what? Why me? I had just walked away from the church. I didn't feel ready for anything, let alone stepping into a spiritual calling that seemed far beyond my understanding.

But the experiences continued, each one more intense than the last. During moments of prayer or meditation, I began to see flashes of light, hear whispers of wisdom that didn't come from my own mind. Sometimes I would be pulled out of my body, my consciousness traveling to places I couldn't describe. I saw heavens, hells, and all things in between—majestic beings whose presence filled me with a peace that was almost overwhelming. I also encountered darkness—malevolent entities that seemed intent on testing my resolve, feeding on my fear.

At first, these encounters terrified me. I didn't know how to navigate them, nor did understand why they were happening. But over time, I began to sense a pattern, a purpose. Each experience seemed designed to teach me something—to show me how to wield the authority I didn't yet know I had.

During my process of discovery, I had a profound teaching moment that would forever change the trajectory of my life. At that time, I was trapped in a cycle of intense sleep paralysis. Night after night, I would be engulfed in terror and helplessness. As someone who could see the spiritual realm, I wasn't just experiencing the paralysis—I could see the malevolent beings that entered my room. They were dark and ugly with ill intentions, closing in on me, threatening to overpower me and intensify my fear. I would panic, my heart racing as I tried to move, but my body was paralyzed, bound by an invisible force. The only thing that could give me any relief was calling out the name of Jesus.

And every time, without fail, the room would fill with a brilliant light, pushing back the shadows, and the dark beings would scatter. It was always the same—until one night, something different happened.

One life-changing night, as I lay in my bed, the darkness felt heavier, more oppressive than usual. A powerful, malicious energy began to fill the room, like a dense fog, and I could feel the malevolent presence pressing in on me. My heart began to race, and I instinctively called out, "Jesus!" But nothing happened. I called again, more urgently, "Jesus!" But again, nothing. The light didn't fill the room. The evil energy didn't dissipate. I was paralyzed in both body and spirit, left in the suffocating grip of fear and confusion.

Then, as clear as day, I heard a voice—the voice of Jesus. It was calm, firm, and full of wisdom.

"I will not be your crutch," the voice said, "I am not your babysitter. I am here to teach you and guide you to reach your full potential in the Body of Christ.

At first, I was stunned. I had always called on Jesus to save me from these forces, to protect me. But this time, it felt like a rebuke—a challenge, almost. Was I leaning too heavily on the idea that Jesus was supposed to save me in every moment of danger, that I was powerless on my own? In that moment, the truth began to sink in.

Then, in a sudden flash of insight, a scripture came to mind, one that had always been a cornerstone of my faith: John 14:12.

"Truly, truly, I say to you, whoever believes in me will also do the works that I do; and greater works than these will he do, because I am going to the Father."

As those words echoed in my mind, the meaning became crystal clear. Jesus wasn't here to constantly save me. His mission was not to be a perpetual protector, always intervening to rescue me from every danger. His mission was to teach me, to help me realize the power that resides within me—to guide me to become a self-sufficient carrier of the Holy Spirit. He came to show me how to operate in the love and power that he embodied.

In that moment, I understood the assignment.

A surge of realization coursed through me, and without thinking, I dug deep within myself. I called upon the love that resides at the core of every soul. I reached within, beyond the fear, beyond the darkness, to tap into the wellspring of divine love that had always been there but that I had never fully harnessed. As I did, something miraculous happened. My body began to glow— radiant, golden light emanated from me, filling the room. A fire surrounded me, not of destruction, but of pure, divine energy. The dark forces that had once ruled over me, that had made their presence known in every corner of the room, began to retreat.

And in that instant, I realized something that would change me forever.

Jesus, as deserving as he is of praise, worship, and reverence for what he did, had never intended to be worshipped in the way we often think. He didn't come simply to be glorified, nor to act as an eternal crutch for us when we were afraid. No, his true mission was to serve, to show us how to live in love, to demonstrate the way of divine consciousness. He came to teach every soul, every one of us, how to step into our own power—to move in the world with the same love, compassion, and divine strength that he embodied.

As John 14:12 says: "Whoever believes in me will also do the works that I do; and greater works than these will he do..." The realization struck me hard—Jesus did not come to be worshipped merely for his miracles; he came to empower us to do greater works, to walk in the fullness of the divine power he carried. This was the message he had been teaching all along. The light and power I had been seeking outside of myself had always been within me.

The light that filled the room that night wasn't just a result of Jesus' intervention. It was the manifestation of something deeper—the awakening of the inner light that he had always wanted us to recognize within ourselves. The love, the power, the healing—it was always available within me. Jesus showed me how to access it.

I thought back to Matthew 17:20, when Jesus told his disciples: "If you have faith like a grain of mustard seed, you will say to this mountain, 'Move from here to there,' and it will move, and nothing will be impossible for you." I had been relying on external forces to move the darkness. But now, I understood that the faith Jesus spoke of was within me, and with even a small amount of faith, I had the power to move mountains. I had the power to cast out darkness from my life.

This realization was reinforced by Romans 8:11: "If the Spirit of him who raised Jesus from the dead dwells in you, he who raised Christ Jesus from the dead will also give life to your mortal bodies through his Spirit who dwells in you." The Spirit of the Living God, the same Spirit that raised Jesus from the dead, lived within me. And with that Spirit came the power to overcome, the power to live in victory, not just in the moments of fear, but always.

From that night on, everything shifted. I understood that I wasn't helpless. I wasn't powerless. I didn't need to wait for external forces to intervene or for someone else to fight my battles. I carried within me the same light that Jesus had, the same power of the Holy Spirit, and I had the ability to call on it, to activate it, to walk in it—whenever I needed it.

That night was no longer a moment of terror or helplessness. It was a lesson. A rebirth.

I had been taught what I needed to know, not just for that moment, but for every moment of my life to come. Jesus didn't just want me to call on him for rescue; he wanted me to step into the full awareness of who I was, of the power within me, and of the divine love that could never be taken from me.

The dark forces that once terrified me no longer had any power over me. I had learned to stand in my own light—and I knew that no matter what challenges I faced, I would never be alone.

As 1 John 4:4 says, "He who is in you is greater than he who is in the world." With this truth, I walked forward into my life with a new understanding of who I am and the divine power that resides within me. The divine power that dwells within us all.

But the journey didn't stop there. What I had experienced that night was just the beginning. This newfound awareness didn't just change the way I responded to fear or spiritual warfare. It shifted the way I lived my daily life. I began to approach every moment with a sense of purpose, knowing that I was never at the mercy of any external force. The challenges I faced became opportunities to step further into the power of the Spirit, to learn how to align my thoughts and actions with divine will.

I stopped waiting for something or someone outside of me to change the circumstances I was in. Instead, I began to understand that the change I was seeking started within. My prayer life became less about asking for protection and more about aligning myself with the abundant life God had promised me—recognizing the authority I had to declare light over darkness, peace over chaos, and healing over brokenness.

I also began to understand that this revelation wasn't just for me. It wasn't a private truth. The power that resides within me also resides within others, waiting to be awakened. This became my mission—to help others realize their own divine potential, to teach them how to tap into the same strength, love, and light that had saved me from my fear.

It was a message of empowerment, not just for the moment of crisis, but for everyday living. We are not meant to live in fear, passively waiting for rescue. We are meant to rise up, to claim our divine inheritance, and to live in the fullness of the Spirit.

I no longer feared the darkness. I now understood that If carried the light within me, that light would never fail.

These experiences were not just random occurrences—they were a kind of sacred schooling. Each encounter taught me something about the spiritual realms and the power I carried as a child of God. I learned that fear was the greatest weapon of darkness, and that love and faith were the antidotes. I learned that the spirit realms were not separate from the physical world but deeply intertwined, each influencing the other in ways I was only beginning to understand.

The more I embraced these lessons, the more my spiritual gifts began to grow. I could see beyond the surface of things, sense the energy that surrounded people and places. I began to recognize when someone was carrying pain, fear, or darkness, and I felt a deep compassion to help them. I didn't fully understand how, but I knew that my journey into the spiritual planes was preparing me for something greater.

Not everyone understood what I was experiencing. When I tried to share my encounters, I was often met with skepticism or fear. Some people dismissed my stories as dreams or hallucinations; others warned me that I was treading dangerous ground. But I knew in my heart that these experiences were real, that they were part of my calling.

In time, I stopped trying to explain myself to others and focused on listening to the divine guidance within me. I began to see my journey not as a burden but as a gift—a chance to grow, to heal, and to help others find their way.

The spiritual plane became my classroom, and each encounter was a lesson in faith, courage, and the boundless power of love. I learned that the battles I faced were not just for my own growth but for the healing of others, for the liberation of those who were bound by fear and darkness. And as I stepped deeper into this calling, I began to see that the answers I had sought as a child—the purpose I had longed to understand—were unfolding before me, one sacred step at a time.

Chapter 5
The Astral Plane and Lessons of Fear

The astral plane was unlike anything I had experienced before. It was a place where the laws of the physical world no longer applied, where thoughts and emotions seemed to take on form and substance. For someone like me, whose spiritual senses were awakening, it felt both fascinating and overwhelming. The more I ventured into this plane of existence, the more I realized how little I understood about it—and how much I had to learn.

At first, my journeys to the astral plane were unintentional. I would slip into this space during sleep or prayer, my consciousness detaching from my physical body and drifting into the ether. The sensation was exhilarating, like floating weightlessly through a vast and infinite omniverse. But it wasn't long before the exhilaration turned to fear.

Dark entities seemed to linger on the edges of my awareness, their presence cold and suffocating. These shadowy figures would draw closer, feeding on the fear that welled up inside me. Each time, I would panic, willing myself to return to my body as quickly as possible. I would wake up trembling, the weight of their energy still clinging to me. I began to dread these experiences, wondering if I was delving into something I wasn't ready for.

It was during one of these encounters that I learned a lesson that would change everything.

One night, I found myself in the astral plane again, standing in a vast, shadowy expanse. The air was thick with a palpable sense of unease. Before me stood a towering figure, its form dark and menacing, its eyes glowing like embers. It exuded a presence that made my knees weak, and every instinct told me to run.

But this time, something was different. Instead of succumbing to fear, I felt a quiet voice rise within me—a voice that reminded me of who I was. *You are a child of light. You have nothing to fear.*

The figure began to advance, its shadow stretching toward me like tendrils. My heart raced, but I didn't retreat. I took a deep breath and focused on the light within me, the divine presence that had carried me through so many trials. As the figure drew closer, I raised my hand and spoke with authority: *You have no power here. Leave! I come under the authority of Jesus.*

In that moment, something extraordinary happened. A light erupted from within me, radiant and golden, flooding the space around me. The figure recoiled, its form unraveling like smoke caught in the wind. The fear that had gripped me dissolved, replaced by a profound sense of peace and strength.

When I returned to my body, I felt a shift in my being. The fear that had once controlled me no longer held the same power. I realized that the entities I had encountered in the astral plane were not invincible—they were fueled by the energy I gave them. The more I feared them, the stronger they became. But when I stood in my authority, when I chose faith over fear, their power dissolved.

This realization marked a turning point in my journey. I began to approach the astral plane with a sense of curiosity and purpose rather than dread. Instead of avoiding the darkness, I learned to face it, to transform it with the light within me. The astral plane, once a place of fear, became a sacred space for growth and healing.

As I gained confidence, I began to explore this realm more intentionally. I discovered that the astral plane was not just a place of conflict but a place of profound connection. I encountered spirits seeking guidance, fragments of lost souls searching for peace. Each interaction taught me something new about the nature of the universe, the power of love, and the interconnectedness of all things.

When I returned to my body, I carried with me a new understanding of the astral plane. It was not a place to be feared but a place to be navigated with wisdom and intention. It was a space where the soul could grow, where healing could take place on levels beyond the physical.

Through these experiences, I came to see fear not as an enemy but as a teacher. It showed me the areas where I needed to grow, the places where I had yet to fully trust in the power of God. By confronting my fears, I learned to step into my spiritual authority, to stand in the light that no darkness could overcome.

The astral plane had tested me, but it had also transformed me. It taught me that the greatest battles are not fought with fists or weapons but with faith, love, and the unwavering belief in the power of light. And it prepared me for the work that lay ahead—the work of healing, guiding, and helping others find their way through the darkness.

Chapter 6
The Pentecostal Shaman

The term *shaman* was not one I had ever associated with myself. Growing up in the Pentecostal tradition, shamanism was something we were taught to avoid—an ancient, mysterious practice that belonged to cultures far removed from the church. Yet, as my spiritual journey deepened, I found myself drawn to the parallels between the two worlds. Pentecostalism had shaped my foundation, but shamanism seemed to offer a bridge to something even broader—a way to connect with the mind of God beyond the constraints of doctrine.

It wasn't an easy path to accept. I wrestled with the implications of what it meant to embrace both identities, to call myself *The Pentecostal Shaman.* At first glance, it seemed like a contradiction, a merging of two worlds that had long stood in opposition. But as I reflected on my experiences, I realized that these two paths were not as separate as I had been led to believe. In fact, they complemented each other in ways that felt profoundly natural.

Pentecostalism was where I first encountered the Holy Spirit, where I learned to move in the rhythm of divine power. I was raised in a tradition that celebrated miracles, spiritual gifts, and the direct presence of God. We were taught to lay hands on the sick, to cast out demons, to pray in tongues, and to surrender ourselves fully to the will of the Spirit. These practices, though rooted in the church, carried a universal truth: the power of the divine flows through us all, and it is our birthright to access it.

But as much as I loved the passion and fervor of Pentecostal worship, I often felt that something was missing. The church emphasized the power of the Spirit but rarely delved into the deeper mysteries of the unseen world. Questions about the nature of the soul, the workings of the spiritual realms, and our connection to the universe were often left unanswered or dismissed as irrelevant. My experiences in the spirit realms, however, told me there was more.

Shamanism, in its essence, is about walking between worlds. It is the practice of stepping into the spiritual realms to bring back wisdom, healing, and transformation for the physical world. When I began to explore this path, I discovered that it mirrored many of the practices I had already been taught in the church. Both traditions spoke of healing, of spiritual authority, and of the ability to access the divine for the benefit of others.

Through my journeys in the spirit realms, I found myself engaging in what could only be described as shamanic practices. I would travel to other planes of existence, guided by Jesus to confront darkness, retrieve lost soul fragments, and bring healing to those in need. These experiences didn't conflict with my faith; they deepened it. They showed me that the power of the Holy Spirit wasn't confined to the walls of a church—it was everywhere, in everything.

The more I embraced this duality, the more I realized that the boundaries between Pentecostalism and shamanism were human constructs. The Spirit moved where it willed, unconcerned with our labels or divisions. What mattered was the intention, the heart behind the work. Whether I was praying in tongues or journeying to the astral plane, the purpose was the same: to bring light, healing, and liberation.

Adopting the title *The Pentecostal Shaman* was an act of reclaiming my truth. It was a declaration that I refused to be confined by the expectations of any one tradition. I honored the Pentecostal fire that had shaped my early faith, but I also embraced the shamanic calling that had awakened within me. Together, these paths formed a holistic understanding of the divine—one that transcended boundaries and brought together the best of both worlds.

Some people struggled to understand this merging of identities. They questioned how I could reconcile the two, given their apparent contradictions. But to me, there was no contradiction at all. Jesus himself walked between worlds, healing the sick, casting out demons, and speaking of truths that defied the conventions of his time. He was, in many ways, a shaman—a bridge between the physical and the spiritual, a guide who showed us how to access the divine power within ourselves.

My work as The Pentecostal Shaman is rooted in this example. It is not about rejecting one tradition for another but about integrating the wisdom of both to serve a higher purpose. It is about recognizing that the divine is too vast to be contained within any one framework. Whether I am laying hands on someone in prayer or journeying to the spirit realms to bring back a lost part of their soul, I am guided by the same force: LOVE.

My mission is to help others find their truth, to guide them toward healing and self-discovery. I work with people from all walks of life, regardless of their faith or background, helping them reconnect with the divine power within themselves. For some, this means breaking free from the constraints of religious dogma. For others, it means confronting the darkness within and reclaiming their light.

I have learned that healing is not about fixing what is broken; it is about remembering wholeness. It is about helping people see that they are already connected to the divine, already capable of accessing the wisdom and power they seek. My role is not to give them the answers but to help them ask the right questions, to guide them as they step into their own authority.

The title *The Pentecostal Shaman* may seem unconventional, but it is a reflection of my journey—one that has taken me beyond the boundaries of tradition and into the boundless freedom of divine love. It is a reminder that we are not defined by labels or limitations but by the love and light we carry within us.

Chapter 7
Miracles Across Planes

Miracles are often thought of as isolated events—rare, extraordinary moments where divine intervention defies the natural order. But through my journey, I've come to understand that miracles are not rare at all. They are always present, waiting for us to align with the divine energy that makes them possible. I've seen miracles unfold in the physical world and across spiritual planes, and each one has deepened my understanding of the interconnectedness of all things.

One of the most profound lessons I've learned is that miracles are not bound by the laws of time, space, or logic. They occur when faith, love, and intention align to create a pathway for divine energy to flow. This understanding has been the foundation of my work as both a healer and a bridge between realms.

One particular miracle stands out the most. I found myself in the astral plane, standing near a stretch of highway near my home. The scene before me was hauntingly vivid: an overturned car lay in a ditch, its frame mangled from the impact of a crash. Two bodies were sprawled on the ground nearby, lifeless and broken. Surrounding them were spirits—family members, I sensed—grieving over their loss. The air was heavy with sorrow and anger, emotions so intense that they seemed to ripple through the fabric of the plane.

I felt a pull to intervene, though I wasn't sure what I could do. As I stepped closer, I began to pray, calling on Jesus for guidance. The spirits turned to me, their faces etched with a mix of hope and desperation. I addressed them gently: *"If you believe in miracles, stay with me. If not, I ask you to step aside and allow the work to be done."*

The energy in the space shifted, and I felt a surge of faith from those who stayed. It was as though their belief created a channel through which healing energy could flow. I knelt beside the bodies, my hands trembling as I placed them on the chest of the first victim. Closing my eyes, I prayed with all the conviction in my heart, commanding life to return.

A radiant blue light emanated from my hands, enveloping the body in its glow. Slowly, I felt the chest rise and fall beneath my palms. The victim's eyes fluttered open, and I could sense the spirits around me erupting in joy. But there was still more work to do.

I moved to the second body, which was dismembered and broken in ways that defied comprehension. This time, I called on the energy of love itself. As I prayed, ants began to emerge from the soil, carrying pieces of the body and placing them together with remarkable precision. The ground shifted, sealing the wounds as though nature itself was participating in the miracle. My hands radiated the same blue light, and with one final prayer, I felt the pulse of life return to the body.

The spiritual family wept with gratitude, their grief transformed into celebration. I stood in awe of what had unfolded, humbled to have been a vessel for such profound healing. When I returned to my physical body, I wondered if the experience had been purely spiritual or if it had somehow impacted the physical world as well.

That morning, as I drove to work, I passed the very stretch of highway I had seen in the astral plane. My heart skipped a beat when I saw the remnants of an accident—the overturned car, the shattered glass—almost like a moment of Deja Vu. Reports later revealed that the two victims had walked away from the crash with nothing more than sore muscles. There were no broken bones, no injuries—nothing that could be explained logically given the condition of the car.

This experience solidified my understanding of the connection between the spiritual and physical realms. What happens in one plane can ripple into the other, creating changes that defy explanation. Miracles, I realized, are not bound by the limitations of our understanding—they are expressions of love and intention.

Miracles like these are not reserved for the chosen few. They are available to all who believe, to all who open themselves to the possibility of divine intervention. My role in these moments is not to take credit for what unfolds, but to create a space where faith and love can work together.

Love has always been at the heart of this work. It is the driving force behind every prayer, every act of healing. When I step into the spiritual realms, it is not with the intention of fixing what is broken but of holding space for the spirit to move. Whether I am guiding a lost soul to peace or helping someone release the weight of trauma, the goal is always the same: to remind them of the love within themselves.

Through my journey, I've come to see that miracles are not always dramatic or instantaneous. Sometimes they are subtle, unfolding over time in ways we don't immediately recognize. A kind word, a moment of forgiveness, a shift in perspective—these, too, are miracles, ripples of divine energy that transform the world around us.

Every person carries the potential for miracles within them. The same divine power that healed the victims of the crash flows through each of us, waiting to be awakened. When we align ourselves with love, faith, and intention, we become vessels for the miraculous, channels through which the divine can work.

The work I do as The Pentecostal Shaman is not about performing miracles for others but about helping them realize their own potential to create and experience them. It is about guiding people to connect with the divine within themselves, to step into their spiritual authority and embrace the boundless possibilities of faith.

Chapter 8
Seraphim's Flame

There are moments in life when the divine reveals itself in ways so profound that they leave an indelible mark on your soul. For me, one such moment came when I encountered the *Divine Fire*. It was an experience that not only transformed my understanding of God but also awakened a gift within me that I could never have anticipated.

It began as an ordinary day, one filled with prayer and reflection. I was seeking a deeper connection with God, asking for clarity and guidance on my path. As I lay in bed that evening, my prayers lingering in my heart, I drifted into a state somewhere between sleep and wakefulness. In that in-between space, something extraordinary happened.

A brilliant, amber-colored light appeared in my room. At first, it was just a ball of fire, floating in the air like a living, breathing presence. It descended slowly, its glow filling every corner of the room, and as it came closer, I realized it was not just a light—it was a being. The fire began to take shape, forming into a humanoid figure with blazing wings that stretched out majestically behind it. Its presence was overwhelming, radiating love, power, and purity.

The angel leaned toward me, and though it did not speak in words, I understood its message clearly: *"I Love You."*

Then, with a tenderness that defied the intensity of its form, the angel kissed my cheek. In that instant, I felt a spark ignite within me, a flame that began to spread throughout my entire body. The fire wasn't painful; it was warm, purifying, and alive. It felt as though the very essence of holiness was coursing through my veins, burning away every doubt, fear, and limitation.

As the fire enveloped me, I felt my spirit lift from my body. I was weightless, suspended in a state of complete surrender. Time seemed to dissolve, and I became one with the light, an infinite presence that encompassed everything. The flame didn't consume me—it transformed me. It was as if every cell in my being was being recharged, realigned with the frequency of Jesus's love.

When I returned to my body, I was forever changed. The fire didn't leave me—it stayed, a constant presence that I could feel flickering within me. It wasn't just a gift; it was a responsibility, a tool I was meant to use for healing and transformation.

In the days that followed, I began to understand the purpose of the flame. It was not just for me—it was a gift to be shared. I discovered that the fire could be called upon in moments of need, a force of protection, purification, and healing. It was as though the divine had entrusted me with a fragment of its power, a reminder that I was never alone.

This gift was tested one night when a dark presence entered my room. I woke to the oppressive weight of a demonic entity, its energy cold and malevolent. It sought to overpower me, to draw me into fear. But as it drew closer, the flame within me erupted, a brilliant light that consumed the darkness in an instant. The demon shrieked and vanished, unable to withstand the fire's purity.

From that moment on, I understood that the fire was not just a symbol—it was a weapon, a living force that could confront and overcome any darkness. It became my tool for spiritual warfare, a tangible expression of the divine love and authority that flowed through me.

The flame also became a source of healing, not just for others but for myself. Whenever I felt weighed down by doubt or pain, I would meditate on the fire, allowing its warmth to cleanse and renew me. It burned away the lies I had believed about myself, the wounds I had carried from my past, and the limitations I had placed on my faith. Each time, I emerged stronger, more aligned with the truth of who I was.

The flame taught me that healing is not always gentle. Sometimes, it requires a purging, a burning away of the old to make room for the new. But in that process of purification, there is a profound beauty—a reminder that even in the fire, we are held by love.

As I embraced this gift, I began to use it in my work with others. Whether I was praying for someone, guiding them through spiritual battles, or helping them release old wounds, the flame was always present. It became a source of strength and comfort, a tangible reminder of the divine power that dwells within us all.

One of the most profound moments of sharing the flame came during a session with a woman who had been carrying the weight of generational trauma. She described feeling as though she was bound by chains, unable to move forward. As I prayed with her, I called upon the fire, seeing its warmth surrounding her. In that moment, I saw the chains begin to dissolve, replaced by a radiant light that filled her entire being. When she opened her eyes, tears streaming down her face, she said she felt free for the first time in her life.

The cleansing fire is not mine. It is a gift that resides within each of us, waiting to be awakened. It is the light of love, the power of faith, and the presence of God that can transform even the darkest places. My role as The Pentecostal Shaman is not to wield the flame as my own but to help others recognize it within themselves.

This fire is a reminder that we are never alone, that the divine is always with us, burning brightly in the depths of our souls. It is a call to step into our power, to embrace the light, and to let it guide us through every trial, every battle, and every moment of transformation.

Chapter 9
The Power of Questioning God

From the time I was a child, I asked questions that others avoided. *Why am I here? What is my purpose?* As I grew older, these questions deepened. I began to wonder about the nature of God, the meaning of suffering, and the limits of the faith I had been taught. At first, I was afraid of these questions. In the church, questioning God was often seen as a lack of faith, a sign of rebellion. But I couldn't ignore the restlessness in my spirit.

Over time, I came to see that questioning wasn't a rejection of faith—it was an invitation to grow deeper into it. Each question I asked opened a door to a greater understanding of the divine, a truth that went beyond the boundaries of what I had been taught. In fact, it was through questioning that I found my way back to God, not as a distant authority but as a living presence within me.

In the church, we were often taught that faith was about obedience. Doubts were discouraged, questions were unwelcome, and the answers we were given rarely left room for exploration. To question was to risk being labeled as faithless or sinful. But the more I suppressed my doubts, the more they festered, and I realized that blind faith wasn't faith at all—it was fear.

I began to see how this approach to faith was rooted in control. By discouraging questions, religious institutions ensured that their followers remained within the confines of their doctrine. But this kind of faith lacked the depth and authenticity I longed for. It was rigid, unable to adapt to the complexities of life or the mysteries of the divine.

I knew I had to break free from this cycle. I needed to embrace my doubts, to wrestle with my questions, and to seek answers that resonated with the truth I felt deep within my soul. It was a terrifying step, but one that ultimately led me to a deeper, more authentic faith.

Through this process, I came to understand that questioning God was not an act of defiance, but an act of faith. It required trust—the trust that the divine could handle my doubts, my fears, and my need for clarity. It was in the questioning that I found my answers, not in the form of rigid doctrines but as living truths that resonated in my heart.

As I embraced the power of questioning, my faith began to transform. It became less about rules and rituals and more about relationship. I stopped seeking God in the confines of tradition and started finding the divine in the everyday—in the quiet moments of reflection, in the beauty of nature, and in the depths of my own soul.

I also began to see the interconnectedness of all spiritual paths. The truths I discovered were not limited to Christianity; they resonated across cultures, traditions, and beliefs. I realized that the divine was not bound by religion but present in every seeking heart. This understanding allowed me to embrace my identity as both a Pentecostal and a shaman, a bridge between the spiritual and the physical, the traditional and the mystical.

Now, I see questioning as an essential part of the spiritual journey. It is through our questions that we grow, that we uncover the layers of truth that lie beneath the surface. When I work with others, I encourage them to ask the questions they've been afraid to voice. *Why do I feel disconnected? What is my purpose? How do I find my way back to the light?*

These questions are not signs of doubt; they are signs of awakening. They are the first steps on the path to healing, transformation, and divine connection. My role is not to provide all the answers but to hold space for the questions, to guide others as they seek their own truth.

One of the greatest revelations I've had is that the answers we seek are often already within us. The divine is not a distant figure handing down decrees; it is a presence that dwells in the depths of our being. When we question, we are not searching for something outside of ourselves— we are uncovering the wisdom and love that have been with us all along.

Questioning is not a weakness; it is a gift. It is a sign that we are alive, engaged, and seeking the fullness of what it means to be human and divine. It is through questioning that we grow closer to God, not as a figure to be feared but as a presence to be experienced.

As I reflect on my journey, I am grateful for every question that has led me to where I am today. Each doubt, each moment of uncertainty, was a stepping stone to greater understanding. And I know that the journey is far from over—there will always be more questions, more truths to uncover.

I invite you to embrace your own questions. Let them guide you, challenge you, and transform you. Trust that the divine is not threatened by your doubts but welcomes them as part of your growth. The answers may not come immediately, but they will come—in the stillness, in the searching, and in the light that shines within you.

Chapter 10
Healing Trauma

Trauma leaves an imprint on the soul, a weight that often feels impossible to carry. It shapes the way we see ourselves, the world, and even God. For years, I carried the weight of my own wounds—betrayal, rejection, and the disillusionment that came from being hurt by those I trusted most. I thought healing meant forgetting, pushing the pain into the background and moving forward. But I soon discovered that true healing requires something much deeper: confronting the wounds, releasing the pain, and reclaiming the light that trauma tries to steal.

Trauma doesn't just affect the mind and body; it can also fragment the soul. It creates shadows in the soul, places where fear, anger, and shame take root. These shadows can cloud our connection to the divine, convincing us that we are unworthy of love, that our pain defines us. For me, this disconnection was one of the hardest aspects of trauma to overcome. Even as I prayed, even as I sought God's presence, there was a part of me that felt distant, as though my pain had built a wall between me and the light.

This disconnection wasn't just internal—it showed up in my relationships, my choices, and my sense of purpose. I found myself repeating patterns of self-doubt and fear, avoiding vulnerability because it felt safer to keep others at a distance. But the safety was an illusion. The walls I built to protect myself only deepened the isolation, leaving me trapped in a cycle of pain.

Healing, I learned, is not a linear journey. It is a process that requires patience, courage, and an openness to confront the parts of ourselves we would rather avoid. For me, the first step was acknowledging the pain I had buried. I had to name the wounds, to look at them honestly and without judgment. This was not easy. It meant revisiting memories I wanted to forget, feeling emotions I had tried to suppress. But it was necessary.

One of the most profound tools in my healing process was prayer and meditation. In those quiet moments of stillness, I invited Jesus into my pain. I asked God to shine light into the darkest corners of my soul, to reveal the truths I had been too afraid to face. And slowly, I began to feel the strongholds start to crumble.

Healing also required forgiveness—not just for those who had hurt me, but for myself. I had to release the guilt and shame I had carried, to understand that my worth was not defined by the actions of others or the mistakes I had made. Forgiveness was not about condoning what had happened; it was about freeing myself from the chains of resentment and anger.

As my spiritual gifts developed, I began to see how trauma exists not just in the physical and emotional realms but in the spiritual realm as well. Trauma fragments the soul, scattering pieces of ourselves that become trapped in the pain of the past. In my work as a healer, I often encountered people who carried these fragments without even realizing it. They described feeling incomplete, disconnected, or stuck, unable to move forward no matter how hard they tried.

Through prayer and journeying into the spirit realms, I learned to retrieve these lost pieces of the soul. It was sacred work, a process of calling back the parts of ourselves that had been left behind in moments of trauma. Each time I guided someone through this process, I saw the transformation that occurred when they were made whole again. The light returned to their eyes, their energy shifted, and they began to walk with a newfound sense of freedom and purpose.

One of the most powerful moments of my own healing came during a journey into the spirit planes. I had been praying and meditating on a childhood memory that had haunted me for years—a moment of betrayal that had left a deep scar on my heart. As I entered the spirit realm, I found myself standing before a younger version of myself, the child I had been when the wound was first inflicted. He looked at me with fear and sadness, his eyes filled with questions I didn't know how to answer.

I knelt before him and took his hands in mine. "I'm here to bring you home," I said. "You don't have to stay in this pain anymore."

The child hesitated, his gaze searching mine for reassurance. Slowly, he reached out and embraced me. As he did, I felt a rush of energy, a sense of wholeness I hadn't known I was missing. When I returned to my body, I felt lighter, freer. That lost piece of my soul had been reclaimed, and with it came a profound sense of peace.

My own journey taught me that healing is not something we do alone. It requires connection—to God, to ourselves, and to others who can hold space for our pain. As I began to walk more fully in my calling, I felt a deep compassion for those who were carrying the weight of trauma. I wanted to help them see that healing was possible, that they were not defined by their pain.

In my work, I often guide people through the process of releasing trauma and reclaiming their love. Whether through prayer, meditation, or journeying into the spirit realms, I create a space where they can confront their wounds and begin to heal. It is sacred work, a reminder that even in our darkest moments, we are never beyond the reach of divine love.

Healing is not just about letting go of pain—it is about rediscovering the truth of who we are. It is about remembering that we are whole, even when life tries to convince us otherwise. The journey is not always easy, but it is always worth it.

Through my own healing, I have come to see trauma not as a curse but as a teacher. It has shown me the strength I carry, the power of forgiveness, and the infinite capacity of the soul to transform. And it has given me the gift of empathy, the ability to walk alongside others on their own paths to healing.

If you are carrying the weight of trauma, know that you are not alone. The light within you is still there, waiting to be uncovered. Healing is possible, and it begins with the courage to face your pain and the faith to believe in your own resilience. Together, we can reclaim the light that trauma tries to steal and step into the fullness of who we are meant to be.

Chapter 11
Full Circle – Returning to Love and Service

When I walked away from the church, I never imagined I would return. The betrayal and pain I experienced left scars that seemed impossible to heal. The walls of the institution that had once been my sanctuary had crumbled, leaving me to rebuild my faith brick by brick, in places far removed from the pews I had known. But as my journey of healing and transformation unfolded, life brought me full circle. I found myself back in the space that had once broken me, not as the wounded soul I had been, but as someone transformed by the power of true love and service.

My personal encounters with divine love had broadened my understanding of what love truly is. It wasn't just an emotion or an obligation—it was an action, a commitment to show up for others in their moments of need, to hold space for their pain, and to guide them toward healing. Love, I learned, was not about perfection but about presence. It was about being there, even when it was hard, and offering what I had learned through my own trials as a gift to others.

Returning to the church wasn't easy. At first, it felt like stepping back into a battlefield. The memories of judgment, betrayal, and hurt resurfaced, threatening to pull me back into old wounds. But something had changed within me. I no longer viewed the church through the lens of bitterness and pain. Instead, I saw it as a place filled with broken people, much like myself, yearning for the light that could heal them.

The experiences I had outside the church—journeys through the spiritual planes, battles with darkness, and encounters with divine love—had given me tools and insights that I now realized were meant to be shared. The church, for all its flaws, was still a place where people gathered to seek God. And where there was seeking, there was an opportunity to serve.

I began to approach my return not as a reunion with an institution but as a mission of love. I wasn't there to prove anyone wrong or to relive old wounds. I was there to serve, to be a vessel for the divine light that had transformed me. I offered my gifts—my ability to pray, to heal, and to guide others—not as a way to reclaim my place in the church, but as a way to show others that healing and divine connection were possible.

The people I encountered were not so different from the version of myself that had once felt abandoned by the church. They carried their own wounds—stories of loss, disillusionment, and unanswered prayers. As I listened to their pain, I saw myself in them, and my heart swelled with compassion. I began to see the church not as an institution but as a collection of individuals, each on their own journey, each searching for something greater than themselves.

One moment stands out as a turning point. A young woman approached me after a service, her eyes brimming with tears. She shared her story of feeling abandoned by

God and betrayed by people she had trusted. Her pain was palpable, and I recognized it as the same pain I had carried for years. I took her hands in mine and said, "I understand. I've been there. But I promise you, healing is possible."

As I prayed with her, I felt the warmth of the divine presence envelop us both. It wasn't just my prayer or my words—it was the light within her, waiting to be awakened, that brought healing into that moment. When she opened her eyes, she smiled through her tears. "Thank you," she whispered. "I feel hope again."

Moments like these reminded me why I had been brought back. The church was not perfect, and it never would be. But it was a place where love could still break through, where healing could still happen, and where I could use the gifts I had been given to make a difference.

True love, I realized, was not about avoiding the places that had hurt us. It was about returning to those places with a new perspective, a new strength, and a new purpose. Love was about service—offering ourselves as instruments of healing and transformation, even in the face of imperfection.

Through my return to the church, I found a deeper understanding of forgiveness. Forgiveness wasn't about condoning what had happened or forgetting the pain—it was about releasing the hold that pain had on my heart. It was about choosing to see the humanity in others, even when they had fallen short, and offering them the same grace that I had received on my journey.

In many ways, my return to the church felt like the completion of a circle. The place that had once been a source of pain had become a place where I could bring healing—not just to others, but to myself. It was a reminder that even our deepest wounds can be transformed into sources of strength and purpose.

As I continued to serve, I found joy in the simple act of being present for others. Whether it was through prayer, listening, or simply standing alongside someone in their moment of struggle, I saw the power of love at work. And I realized that my journey, with all its twists and turns, had prepared me for this very moment.

Returning to the church didn't erase the pain of the past, but it transformed it. It showed me that love is not about avoiding brokenness but about stepping into it with an open heart, ready to bring light where it is needed most. And in doing so, I found that the light within me burned even brighter.

As The Pentecostal Shaman, I now serve not just as a healer or a guide but as a bridge—between past and present, pain and healing, tradition and transformation. My journey has brought me full circle, and I stand ready to serve wherever I am needed, guided by the power of love.

Chapter 12
Awakening to Your Divine Potential

Every person carries within them an immense reservoir of divine love, a spark of the infinite that connects them to the Creator and to all of existence. Yet, for so many of us, this potential lies dormant, buried beneath fear, doubt, and the weight of the world's expectations. Awakening to your divine potential is not about becoming someone else—it is about remembering who you already are.

From a young age, I sensed that there was more to life than what I could see or touch. This awareness was the beginning of my journey toward understanding the divine light within me. For years, I sought this light in the teachings of the church, in the guidance of mentors, and in the wisdom of sacred texts. But it wasn't until I looked inward that I truly began to see it.

The light within us is not something we have to earn—it is our birthright. It is the essence of who we are, the spark of the divine that animates our being. When we awaken to this truth, we begin to see ourselves not as separate or limited but as part of something infinite and eternal.

One of the greatest barriers to awakening is the belief that we are powerless. Society, religion, and even our own minds often tell us that we are small, that we must rely on external forces to save us or make us whole. But this belief is a lie—a chain designed to keep us from stepping into our power.

Breaking free from these chains requires courage. It means confronting the narratives that have kept us bound, questioning the beliefs that no longer serve us, and trusting in the divine power that flows through us. For me, this process was both liberating and terrifying. It meant letting go of the safety of tradition and stepping into the unknown. But in doing so, I discovered a freedom and strength I never knew existed.

Awakening to your divine potential is not just about recognizing your light—it is about learning to walk in it. This means embracing your spiritual authority, understanding that you are not at the mercy of circumstances or external forces. You have the power to create, to heal, and to transform your reality.

For me, stepping into this authority meant learning to trust myself and the guidance of the divine. It meant speaking life into situations that seemed hopeless, standing firm in the face of darkness, and believing in the power of miracles. Each step I took in faith strengthened my connection to the divine and deepened my understanding of the limitless potential within me.

Awakening to your divine potential is not a destination—it is a way of being. It is about living in alignment with your true self, embracing the light within you, and allowing it to shine through everything you do. When you live in this alignment, you become a beacon of hope, love, and transformation for those around you.

This doesn't mean life will always be easy. Challenges will still arise, but you will face them with a newfound strength and resilience. You will see obstacles not as barriers but as opportunities to grow and expand. And you will begin to understand that the divine power within you is greater than anything you could ever face.

As you reach this point in the journey, I invite you to reflect on the truth of who you are. You are not small. You are not powerless. You are a divine being, connected to the Creator and to all of existence. The light within you is waiting to be uncovered, to be embraced, to be shared with the world.

Awakening to your divine potential is not a one-time event—it is a lifelong process of discovery, growth, and transformation. Each step you take, no matter how small, brings you closer to the fullness of who you are meant to be.

So take the step. Ask the questions. Confront the fears. Trust in the light within you. And know that as you awaken to your divine potential, you are not alone. The Creator walks with you, guiding you every step of the way.

As I reflect on this journey, I am filled with gratitude—not only for the moments of clarity and triumph but also for the challenges and uncertainties that shaped me. Every question, every battle, every revelation has brought me closer to the truth: that the light we seek is already within us, waiting to be uncovered and embraced.

This book has been a labor of love, a testament to the power of faith, healing, and transformation. It is not just my story; it is an invitation—a call to remember the divine light that dwells in each of us.

The path of awakening is not linear. It twists and turns, rises and falls, and sometimes leads us into the depths before lifting us into the heights. But every step, no matter how difficult, is sacred. Every challenge is an opportunity to grow, to shed what no longer serves us, and to step into the fullness of who we are meant to be.

As you close these pages, know that your journey is just beginning. Whether you are standing in the light or still searching for it, you are exactly where you are meant to be. Trust the process, honor your questions, and have faith in the divine presence that guides you.

My hope is that this book has offered you more than inspiration—that it has offered you tools, insights, and a deeper connection to the divine within you. The light you carry is unique, powerful, and needed in this world. As you awaken to your divine potential, you become a beacon for others, showing them what is possible.

You are not alone on this journey. Every step you take brings you closer to the Creator, closer to your true self, and closer to the infinite love that surrounds us all. Together, we walk in the light, guided by the divine, united by our shared humanity and divinity.

As you move forward, may you carry these truths with you:

You are deeply loved, especially when you embody love.

The light within you is powerful and eternal.

Healing, transformation, and miracles are always possible.

May you walk boldly in your divine authority, embracing your questions, your growth, and your infinite potential. And may the Creator's love guide you, now and always, as you continue to awaken to the truth of who you are.

Thank you for allowing me to share this journey with you. May your path be filled with light, love, and endless discovery.

Made in the USA
Columbia, SC
24 November 2024